Sloths
For Kids

Amazing Animal Books
For Young Readers

By
Rachel Smith

Mendon Cottage Books
JD-Biz Corp Publishing

All Rights Reserved.

No part of this publication may be reproduced in any form or by any means, including scanning, photocopying, or otherwise without prior written permission from JD-Biz Corp

Copyright © 2015. All Images Licensed by Fotolia and 123RF.

Read More Amazing Animal Books

Purchase at Amazon.com

.

Table of Contents

Introduction

You've probably heard of someone being called a sloth, or even of one of the Seven Deadly Sins, Sloth.

But what is a sloth, and how did it come to be used as a bad thing to be called? You might guess that it's some sort of horrible animal, but the truth couldn't be any different.

Sloths are slow creatures, named for the sin rather than the other way around. However, there is nothing wrong with being slow, and as you'll see, they are quite loveable creatures that cause harm to almost no one (other than things like insects).

What is a sloth?

Sloths belong to the order Pilosa. However, not all animals in the order are sloths; instead, they belong to two families within the order: Megalonychidae and Bradypodidae. Any animal in those two families is a sloth.

A mama sloth and a baby sloth.

However, there are other sloths that are long extinct, known as ground sloths. Back many years ago, when many gigantic creatures roamed the earth, these sloths were enormous and couldn't climb trees due to their size. Some of them were the size of modern day elephants!

There were even sloths that lived part of the time or most of the time in the water, eating seaweed and the like. These were enormous too.

However, sloths nowadays are more of a medium size, not small but not large either. They have fur covering their bodies, and long arms. They eat only things like leaves and shoots, which means they are folivores, though some kinds eat bugs, small birds and reptiles, and sometimes even human feces (also called poop).

Since most live off of leaves and the like, a food source which is low in calories and not easy to digest, they tend to have to eat a lot. Also, a sloth has a huge stomach with a lot of bacteria in it. The bacteria helps break down the food, though the process of digesting the leaves can take as long as a month. A sloth that is eating well weighs more, as much of its body weight is what's in its stomach.

Sloths have very long tongues. They can stick them out about ten to twelve inches out of their mouth; if you were to measure the average human's, it might be somewhere around three inches or less. These tongues help them grab food and eat it.

They move around in trees, hanging from their limbs. Because they get so little nutrients from their food, they have to use it wisely. This means they move very slowly, eating as they go. This also means that they have a low metabolic rate, which means they use energy more slowly.

Sloths also have a low body temperature; it's even lower when they're resting. All this means that they can survive on non-nutritious food such as the leaves they eat.

Since they require outside heat, in some ways, to keep from being too cold, and a wide range, sloths don't do well outside of the rainforest or jungle. They really can't survive in places like the United States of America, Germany, or China without special preparations. You can't put food in a bowl and expect them to eat it, or even water.

However, sloths do very well within their habitats. Out of the six kinds, four are not endangered at all, in fact thriving. Two kinds are endangered or critically endangered.

Sloths live in Central and South America. They live in the jungles and rainforests, which make an excellent habitation with their thick tree coverage. A sloth can move from branch to branch for the entirety of their lives in a habitat like this, never having to worry about running out of food.

In Brazil, a very large country in South America, there is an issue with deforestation (the loss of trees because humans are cutting them down or things like that) taking away the sloth's home, as well as other animals' homes. This is an issue throughout the world, because human beings need wood for many things, and they also want to build things where the animals' habitats are.

Sloths are actually sort of a habitat of their own. Their fur grows away from their extremities, pointing towards the ground. This is because the sloth spends most of its life hanging upside down, and the way the fur grows protects it better. The fur has one or two kinds of algae that grow on it, and it makes a home for many little tiny creatures to live in. The algae makes a camouflage for the sloth, which means this is a good relationship for both creatures.

For protection, a sloth has curved claws. However, sloths don't usually have much trouble with predators, because they blend in and they move slowly so that they aren't noticed.

The biggest predators of sloths are jaguars, harpy eagles, and humans. Humans are poachers of sloths.

However, electrical lines often cause sloth deaths too. This can be seen as humans causing these deaths too, but not with intent to do it like with poachers.

Sloths are surprisingly good swimmers. As previously mentioned, there used to be a whole kind of large sloths that swam to get their food, and it appears that some of the big ground sloths swam to islands and places like that to colonize. Nowadays, your average sloth can swim very well and has little trouble with water.

As mentioned, sloths move very slowly. They have only a quarter of the muscle of other animals who are the same size. Most of the time, they don't move fast at all, but when they are in danger or something similar, they can move at rates of 13 feet a minute. However, they try not to do this as it burns a lot of energy.

Sloths were once thought to sleep most of the day, but it seems they actually only sleep less than ten hours. Certain kinds are diurnal, which means they're active during the day, like humans, and other kinds are nocturnal, meaning they're active during the night, like bats.

When they need to urinate or defecate (pee or poop), sloths go to the ground at the same spot every time. However, they only do this about once a week.

The reasons why they do this may be many. There is a lot of danger in a sloth being on the ground, as they're much easier to get to for predators, and they have little defense.

One reason may be because falling droppings may attract the attention of predators. Sloths don't bother with going to the ground to urinate during storms, instead doing it where they are.

Another reason may be to help the moths that live in their fur. The mother moth can lay eggs in the feces when the sloth goes to the ground; the moth helps the sloth by providing food for the algae that grows in their fur.

They may also be helping the tree they live on continue to grow and be fertile. Sloths tend to stay in the same tree for a long time.

The last reason may be that leaving the feces and urine there, particularly leaving the tree, may help them find mates. Sloths have a difficult time finding mates, and they need all the help they can get.

Sloths don't mate often, mostly because they can't find each other easily. When they do mate, there is generally one baby, and the baby clings to the mother's fur.

It's said that sometimes the baby will fall, and the mother won't go get it for fear of being killed. However, this may or may not be true.

It's also said that sometimes, sloths will think their own limbs are tree branches and grab onto them, thereby falling from the tree.

In both of these cases, sloths often survive.

What kinds of sloths are there?

There are two main kinds, the two families mentioned before. First, there's the two-toed sloths, of which there are two. Then there are the three-toed sloths, of which there are four.

A three-toed sloth in a tree.

Two-toed sloths and three-toed sloths are not closely related. Their last common ancestor was a creature that living over 35 million years ago, and since then they've mostly been separate creatures.

One kind, the two-toed sloth, is nocturnal. Three-toed sloths are diurnal.

Why are they each called by two-toed and three-toed? While both actually have three toes on their feet, the difference is that two-toed sloths have two fingers on their hands, and three-toed have three.

It's believed that two-toed sloths are closely related to some of the ground sloths that lived a long time ago. Scientific evidence backs this up, and they are actually more closely related to these ground sloths than they are to three-toed sloths! There are a number of these ground sloths in the family, though they are extinct.

Three-toed sloths, on the other hand, have no known very close relatives. Scientists are still looking for links between this kind of sloth and other sloths.

There are three other families of sloths, big ones, that are all extinct. The world used to be far more diverse in sloths, but when the environment changed long, long ago, the mega fauna (big, prehistoric animals) died out or adapted. An example of mega fauna adapting would be the moose, which has survived mostly unchanged since way back then.

As is the rule with nature: if you can't survive, you go extinct.

Relatives of sloths

There are a number of relatives of sloths. This mostly means that they are related to anteaters, and more distantly to armadillos.

A giant anteater.

Anteaters are a South American animal that eats insects, mostly ants. They belong to the order Pilosa, the only other kind of the group. There are about four kinds of anteaters, the silky anteater all on its own in its own family, and the other three in their own family.

One thing that visually links anteaters and sloths are their claws. They both have big, curved claws that are there to protect them.

Another thing is the tongue. Anteaters also have long tongues, though they use them to eat insects.

Armadillos are more distantly related, also a member of the superorder Xenarthra. The superorder contains both the armadillo order and the order Pilosa.

There has been confusion in the past about what animal is related to what. At one point, aardvarks, pangolins, and other animals were groped in with the anteaters and sloths. At another, they were separated.

Basically, there is a lot of debate about orders and superorders. A lot of confusion was there when South American animals started to be put into categories. This is because it was coming from a Western point of view, and there were a lot of animals to figure out. Even nowadays, there are many animals undiscovered by scientists in the rainforest.

The history of sloths and humans

Like most exotic animals, sloths are hunted by poachers. Poachers kill them and take them back to sell them to rich buyers.

A two-toed sloth hanging on a tree branch.

One of the problems for poachers is that often, if they shoot a sloth, it may die, but its hooked claws hold onto the branch anyway. But sloths are easiest to get when they are on the ground, so this is the way poachers most like to catch them. Poachers are one of the biggest predators of sloths, and cause the most recorded deaths, along with electric lines.

Aviaros Sloth Sanctuary, in Costa Rica, takes care of injured or sick sloths. Their job is to heal them and then release them back into the wild. They've done this with over a hundred sloths, a good counterexample to the poachers.

Sloths became somewhat popular since the character of a prehistoric ground sloth in the Ice Age movies was introduced. Before that, it was incredibly rare to even hear of sloths in media, but this sloth made for an interest in sloths. He stands upright, which is not really correct, but he does have the claws one would expect.

Another movie, The Croods, had a sloth in it too, also a prehistoric sloth. This one was a pet, and functioned as a belt for a character.

Thanks to both these movies, the sloth has become somewhat more prominent in media in the 21st century.

Pygmy three-toed sloth

Pygmy three-toed sloths are the most endangered kind of sloth. It is also known as a monk sloth or a dwarf sloth. They are a type of three-toed sloth, closely related to the brown-throated sloth.

Pygmy sloths are significantly smaller than their three-toed relatives. They can be almost half the size of their cousins, the brown-throated sloths.

This is because, back about 8900 years ago, the island they lived on split from the main land. This meant that they were stuck on a small island with a small gene pool. So, eventually, dwarfism as a gene took over and led to smaller sloths.

This type of sloth only eats red mangrove tree leaves. These have less nutrition than what some other sloths eat, but since they are smaller, they can survive on it.

There were only about 70 of them at the last count, which may have been inaccurate. The problem is that they only have a small area to live in, since they only live in mangrove trees. They don't have predators, but it's suspected that the local fishermen will poach them because they're easy targets.

The pygmy sloth is protected by law, but this protection is very lax. This means that anyone who wanted to poach them could do it without being in trouble for it, unless a lot of people started doing it.

There is the hope that there will be something done to save it, as it is very endangered, but so far there is not much being done.

Hoffman's two-toed sloth

Hoffman's two-toed sloth is named for Karl Hoffmann, a German naturalist. Naturalists studied animals.

A Hoffman's sloth.

This sloth is nocturnal, as a two-toed sloth, and it lives in mature and secondary rainforests. This means it lives in fully grown rainforests, and in some that aren't quite there yet.

This type of sloth moves faster than the three-toed sloths, and it has several other differences too. For one thing, it has no hair on the soles of its feet, unlike three-toeds, and its toes aren't partially fused together on its front feet, or hands.

Another example is that its snout is longer and it is larger.

Linnaeus's two-toed sloth is very closely related, and they are often confused for each other. They only have a few differences, mostly in their skeletons.

They have stubby tails, but you can't see them because of how shaggy their fur is. Their fur is tan or light brown, but it often looks green thanks to the algae that grows in it. Around the face, it is a lighter color.

There are five recognized subspecies of Hoffman's two-toed sloth, all in different areas in South America, such as Peru. There are small differences between these subspecies, and a typical person would probably not be able to tell them apart.

There are two general areas that these sloths live. These two areas are wide spreads of rainforest separated from each other.

The interesting thing is that when the two-toed sloth shares an area with three-toed sloths, usually they don't compete with each other, but rather share the space pretty equally, and both dominate it.

This sloth often, whether it means to or not, spits when it opens its mouth. Spittle usually gathers on its bottom lip.

They have poor senses of hearing and sight, and this means they rely heavily on touch and smell.

Brown-throated sloth

The brown-throated sloth is one of the best known kinds of sloth. The reason for this is that it is the most common out of the four kinds of three-toed sloths.

A young brown-throated sloth.

Male and female sloths generally look alike; in fact, it's happened quite a few times that a zoo (specially equipped to take care of sloths) has received a sloth of the wrong gender.

These sloths have peg-like teeth, and no incisors or canines, which are teeth that humans have. Instead, since they don't need to tear meat or other things in the same way, their teeth are just designed to grind.

You can't really see the sloth's ears, though they do have them. They also have a short snout, but their sense of smell is much, much better than their sense of hearing.

The coarse fur of the sloth has many tiny cracks in it, and it's through these cracks that creatures and algae get in. They live there happily, a mini ecosystem within the sloth's fur.

A young sloth doesn't immediately get algae in its fur, and a very old sloth may have lost their algae because their hairs are broken.

A lot of this sloth's habitat overlaps with the Hoffman's two-toed sloth, though because they operate at different hours and don't generally bother each other, they both do well anyway. There are usually more brown-throated sloths than there are Hoffman's two-toed sloths.

This type of sloth looks very similar to its relative the pale-throated sloth, and early on, they were often confused. However, modern science has determined a difference, and so they are classified as separate species.

The interesting thing about the brown-throated sloth is that it doesn't just live in rainforests. Instead, it also lives in evergreen forests (like pine trees) and in forests that are known as 'dry forests,' meaning not rainforests. It is all across South America and parts of Central America.

Mother sloths of this kind carry their babies in their bellies for about seven months. Then, after the baby is born, it stays with her for another five months. For about four to five weeks of that, it nurses. What's interesting about the mother is that, unlike other nursing animals, she doesn't store milk, and instead it is generated as the baby suckles.

The baby suckles almost nonstop for four to five weeks, though, so that makes more sense. As early as four days of age, the baby sloth is already licking its mother's mouth to pick up crumbs of her food. This is how it learns to identify what leaves to eat.

There are seven subspecies of this sloth, but again, it would take someone very experienced to tell most of them apart, and even then, there are some that nearly impossible to tell apart.

Giant sloth

The megatherium is one example of a giant sloth. It was easily as large as an elephant, weighing up to four tons, and it was the tallest animal in South America.

A megatherium, also known as a giant ground sloth.

Before the Panama Isthmus (which is kind of a land bridge) formed, connecting Central America and South America, many kinds of animals flourished in South America.

This included over ten types of ground sloths, but the most notable is the megatherium. The megatherium was not able to climb trees, but since it was so tall, it just stood up on its hind legs and ate the tops of trees. There was no real competition for these areas, since nothing else was as tall as the megatherium.

Mammoths were some of the only animals to be anywhere near its size. Another animal that ended up near its size, an ancestor of the rhinoceros, was the paraceratherium, which was enormous, but lived in Asia.

The Great American Exchange happened after the Panama Isthmus was formed. This didn't really affect ground sloths, though many other animals went extinct when the North American animals came down into South America. Several kinds of animals from South America went up to North America too.

The megatherium, along with other ground sloths, lost its habitat around ten thousand years ago due to changing climate. It's also suggested that human hunting led to their extinction.

Conclusion

The sloth is a very interesting creature indeed. As you can see, it is not a lazy creature, but instead an animal that practices energy conservation (saving energy).

It might be good to take a page out of the sloth's book every so often; human beings just keep going faster and faster, and everyone, no matter who they are, needs a break sometimes.

The sloth will probably continue far into the future, and live thousands of years longer than its cousins the ground sloths. Hopefully, they will never be disturbed from their peaceful lifestyle.

Author Bio

Rachel Smith is a young author who enjoys animals. Once, she had a rabbit which was very nervous, and chewed through her leash and tried to escape. She's also had several pet mice, who were the funniest little animals to watch. She lives in Ohio with her family and writes in her spare time.

Publisher

JD-Biz Corp

P O Box 374

Mendon, Utah 84325

http://www.jd-biz.com/

Sloths   Page 32

Made in the USA
Middletown, DE
21 February 2020

85128571R00020